Dred Scott
and the Supreme Court

by Daniel Rosen

Table of Contents

Introduction.................................... 2

Chapter 1 Dred Scott, Slave....................... 6

Chapter 2 The Fight for Freedom Begins 10

Chapter 3 The Case and the Decision 16

Chapter 4 Reaction and Importance 24

Conclusion 30

Glossary....................................... 31

Index 32

Introduction

The United States was founded in 1776 as a land of freedom. However, by the 1850s, there were more than three million enslaved African Americans in the United States.

Slaves had no rights. They were bought and sold at slave markets. Many times, members of the same family were sold to different owners.

It was illegal for slaves to be taught how to read or write. Slave owners feared that if slaves could read and write, they might resist being held as slaves.

▲ Cotton was one of the main crops grown on plantations.

Most slaves lived on **plantations**, or large farms, in Southern states. Many of the slaves on the plantations worked in fields, planting and harvesting crops. Others lived in the house of their master. Some took care of the house, while others took care of the master's children.

Slave owners were free to treat slaves however they liked. Some owners treated slaves well. Others were cruel and beat their slaves.

Some African Americans in the North lived in freedom. They did not have the same rights as white citizens. Yet many had success in business. Some became leading citizens in their communities.

▲ **Many enslaved workers were needed to grow and harvest the cotton.**

By the 1830s, Northern states had outlawed slavery. Most Northerners did not object to slavery in the South. However, a small group of Northerners did object. They let everyone know their views.

These people were called **abolitionists** (a-buh-LIH-shun-ists) because they wanted to abolish, or outlaw, slavery. One abolitionist leader was an escaped slave named Frederick Douglass.

POINT

Visualize

Imagine a meeting called by Frederick Douglass. Who might he invite? What might they discuss? What plans might they make?

▲ Frederick Douglass

Any actions against slavery upset Southerners. People in the South saw slavery as an important part of the region's economy. They feared that Congress would make laws outlawing slavery. Southerners began to wonder if they could stay part of the United States.

One slave stood up to the law and demanded his right to freedom. His name was Dred Scott. In this book, you will learn how this man's struggle played a key role in changing slavery. You will learn how the case of one slave went all the way to the Supreme Court.

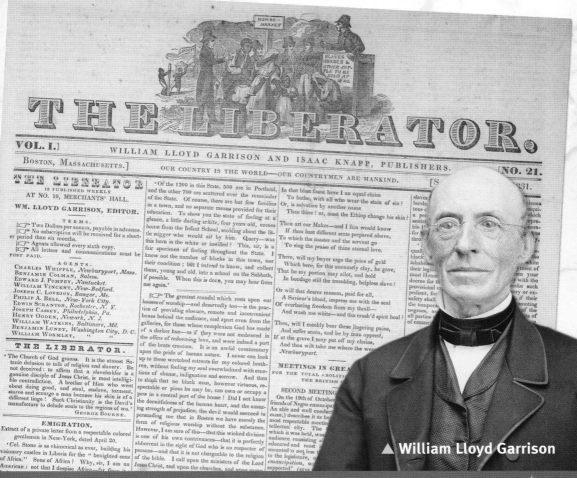

▲ William Lloyd Garrison

▲ William Lloyd Garrison was a leading abolitionist in the North.
He published this newspaper, *The Liberator*.

5

Dred Scott, Slave

Dred Scott was born into slavery around 1800 in Virginia. Both of his parents were slaves. Scott was owned by a man named Peter Blow. The Blow family moved to St. Louis, Missouri, where Peter Blow bought a hotel. In 1830, Blow died. Then Dred Scott was sold to an army doctor named John Emerson.

Math Matters

Total Population in 1850   23,200,000
Number of Slaves in 1850   3,200,000

Of the more than 23 million people living in the United States in 1850, about 14% were enslaved African Americans.

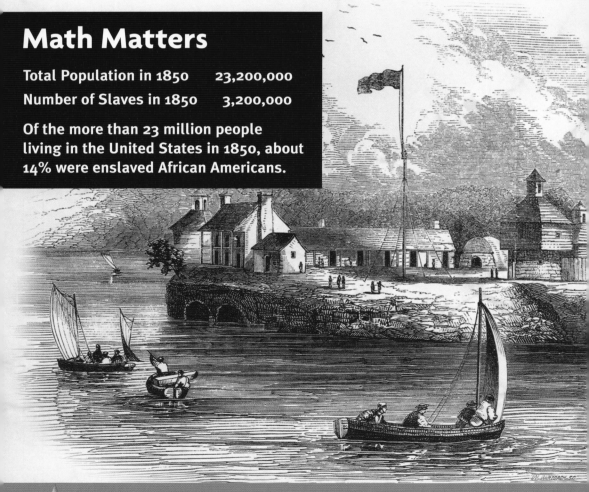

▲ Dr. Emerson reported to Fort Armstrong in Illinois. Illinois was a free state.

In 1833, Dr. Emerson was ordered to report for duty to Fort Armstrong in Illinois. This was an important event in the court case that made Dred Scott famous. Missouri was a **slave state**. Illinois was a **free state**. Slavery was legal in slave states. It was illegal in free states.

In 1836, Dr. Emerson was ordered to move again. This time he went to the Wisconsin **Territory**. A territory was land that belonged to the federal government but was not yet a state. Emerson brought along his slave, Dred Scott. Slavery was illegal in the Wisconsin Territory.

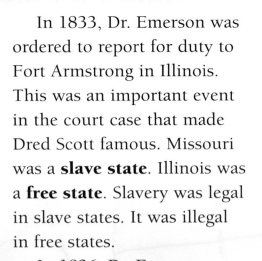

Dred Scott ▶

Dred Scott's Family

Around 1836, Dred Scott met and married Harriet Robinson. She was also a slave. Harriet's owner was a justice of the peace. He performed the wedding ceremony.

Dr. Emerson bought Harriet from her owner. The young Scott family continued to move to different army posts. In the next few years, Dred and Harriet had two daughters. Dr. Emerson married a woman named Irene Sanford.

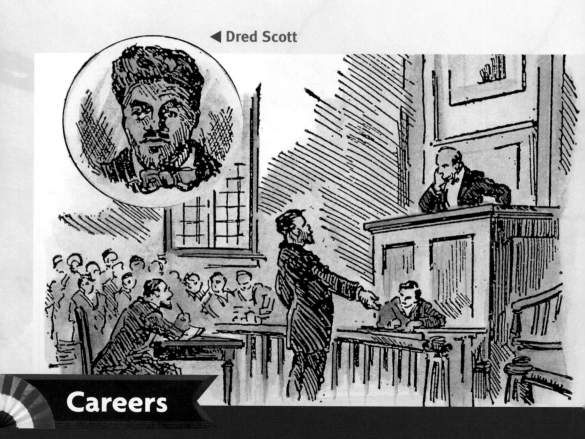

◀ Dred Scott

Careers

Lawyers work with the law. They draw up agreements called contracts. They help people go to court to protect their rights. To become a lawyer, a person needs to attend law school.

The Emersons and Scotts moved to the Iowa Territory in 1842. It, too, was a free territory. A year later, Dr. Emerson died. Irene Emerson moved to St. Louis, taking the Scotts with her. An army captain paid Irene Emerson so he could employ Dred Scott. The Scotts did not like that arrangement. Dred Scott offered to pay Irene Emerson $300 for his freedom, but she refused the offer.

In 1846, Dred Scott filed a **lawsuit** against Irene Emerson in a St. Louis court. The Scott family claimed that they had lived for many years in free territory. Therefore, they could no longer be considered slaves.

▲ Harriet Scott

▲ Roswell Martin Field was a lawyer for Dred Scott.

The Fight for Freedom Begins

When Dred Scott filed his lawsuit, little did he know his would last for eleven years. It went through four different courts. Many lawyers and judges worked on Scott's bid for freedom. The lawyers based their arguments on laws and past court decisions.

Historical Perspective

Continental Congress

The first government of the United States was the Continental Congress. It lasted from 1776 until 1787. The rules for that government were called the Articles of Confederation. By 1787, most Americans felt the old government was not doing a good job of governing the country. Leaders met to write new rules for a new government. The Continental Congress is best remembered for two things: the Declaration of Independence and the Northwest Ordinance. Today, the United States has Congress. It is made up of the House of Representatives and the Senate. It makes laws for the United States.

The Northwest Ordinance was one of the most important laws affecting Scott's case. The law was passed in 1787. It was one of the first laws passed in the United States. It had several parts. It set up the Northwest Territory. Over time, five states were formed from this territory: Ohio, Indiana, Michigan, Illinois, and Wisconsin. The Northwest Ordinance banned slavery in the Northwest Territory. That was why Illinois and the Wisconsin Territory were free. Dred Scott's lawyers argued in court that Scott had lived in an area where slavery was illegal. Therefore, he should no longer be a slave.

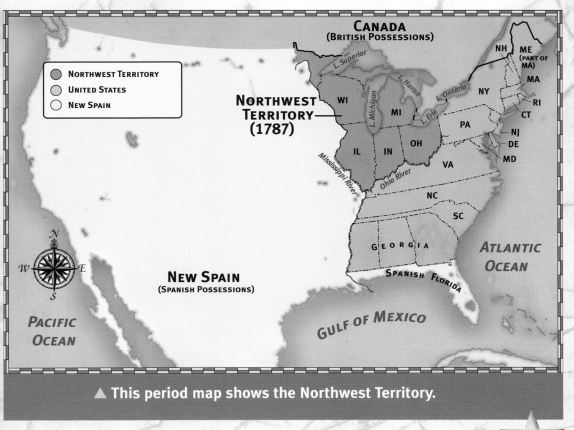

▲ This period map shows the Northwest Territory.

Missouri Compromise

Dred Scott's lawyers also used a law called the Missouri **Compromise** to argue for Scott's right to be free. This law was passed in 1820. A compromise is an argument that is settled when both sides agree to give up something they want.

In 1819, the United States faced a **crisis**, or turning point, over slavery. Missouri was asking to be admitted as a state. Slavery was legal in Missouri. At that time, there were twenty-two states in the United States. Eleven were slave states. Eleven were free states. If Missouri were admitted, that would give the slave states a majority.

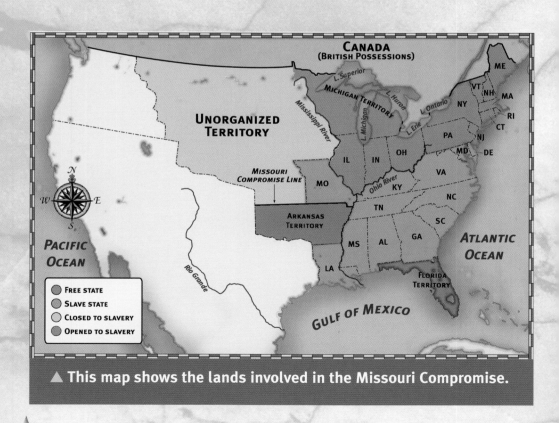

▲ This map shows the lands involved in the Missouri Compromise.

Henry Clay, a congressman from Kentucky, came up with a solution to the problem.

Maine was not a separate state. It had been a part of Massachusetts since colonial times. Slavery was illegal in Maine. Clay suggested that Maine should be admitted to the Union at the same time as Missouri. That way, the balance, between free and slave states would be preserved.

The Missouri Compromise was important for another reason. It banned slavery in all land north of Missouri's southern border, except for Missouri itself. So when Dred Scott lived in the Iowa Territory with the Emersons, he was living in free territory.

They Made a Difference

Henry Clay was one of the greatest political leaders of his time. Clay served in the U.S. Congress as both a representative and senator from Kentucky for almost forty years. He ran for president four times but was never elected. He is best remembered for his efforts to settle the disagreements about slavery between the North and South.

Going to Court

Going to court costs money. Dred Scott was helped by his former owners, the Blow family. The children of Peter Blow were leading citizens in St. Louis. They were opposed to slavery. They gave money to Dred Scott and hired lawyers to help him.

In 1847, Scott went to trial for the first time. Scott's lawyers thought the law was on their side. There had been several other cases in which slaves had been granted freedom after living in free territory. The judge found in favor of Irene Emerson. But he let Scott **appeal** the decision. An appeal is a request to have a legal case heard again by a higher court. So in 1850, another Missouri court heard Scott's case. This time, the judge found in favor of Scott. Dred Scott thought he had won his freedom. But the fight wasn't over. Irene Emerson decided to appeal.

Dred Scott's trial was ▶ held in the Old Court House in St. Louis, Missouri.

In 1852, the Supreme Court of Missouri heard Dred Scott's case. This was the third trial. The Missouri Supreme Court was made up of three judges. By 1852, the country was again swept up by a crisis over slavery. Dred Scott lost his case by a vote of 2–1. The two judges who voted for Irene Emerson did not decide the case based on the law. They let their pro-slavery political views decide the case for them.

Primary Source

The Missouri Supreme Court had once freed many slaves who had spent time in free states. The state followed the rule of "once free, always free." But by the time of Dred Scott's case, the court said, "Times now are not as they were when the previous decisions on this subject were made."

court paper sent to ▶
Irene Emerson

The Case and the Decision

In the 1850s, the issue of slavery was tearing the country apart. People in the North wanted to limit slavery in new territories. Some people wanted to ban it.

But Southerners depended on slavery for their way of life. They wondered if they could still stay part of the United States if laws restricted slavery.

They Made a Difference

Harriet Tubman was born a slave in Maryland. When she was nineteen, she escaped to freedom in the North. Tubman became a guide on the Underground Railroad. The Underground Railroad was a system of escape routes for slaves to find freedom in the North. Tubman led more than 300 slaves to freedom. She said, "I never lost a passenger."

Harriet Tubman ▷

In 1852, a white woman named Harriet Beecher Stowe wrote a novel called *Uncle Tom's Cabin*. It was the story of how slaves were cruelly treated by their owners. Stowe's novel became a best seller. It helped convince many people in the North that slavery was evil. But Southerners were angry at what they saw as an unfair picture of slavery.

In the Kansas Territory, fights broke out between pro-slavery and anti-slavery settlers. Slavery was a big issue in every election. Americans wondered if their country could hold together.

◀ **Harriet Beecher Stowe**

Federal Court

In 1853, Dred Scott's lawyers appealed in federal court. The case had become well known. Many people were interested in the outcome. Abolitionist leaders gave money to Dred Scott to hire a famous lawyer. He hired Montgomery Blair, a Maryland politician and lawyer.

By 1853, Irene Emerson had tired of the court fights. She turned the case over to her brother, John Sanford. He was a New York businessman. A person working at the court misspelled Sanford's name. So the case became known as *Scott v. Sandford*. (The *v* stands for *versus*, a Latin word that means "against.")

▲ Dred Scott signed his name with an X.

▲ Montgomery Blair

John Sanford also hired a famous lawyer. The lawyer, Reverdy Johnson, later became a U.S. senator. The federal court decided the case in favor of Sanford. The judges said that slaves did not have the right to sue in court. That meant that Scott did not have the right to sue in federal court because he was a slave.

There was only one court left for Dred Scott. That was the United States Supreme Court. In 1856, the lawyers argued Scott's case for freedom once again.

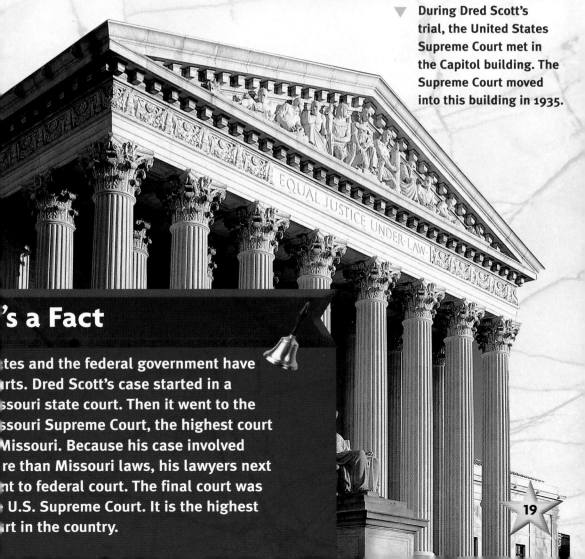

▼ During Dred Scott's trial, the United States Supreme Court met in the Capitol building. The Supreme Court moved into this building in 1935.

's a Fact

tes and the federal government have rts. Dred Scott's case started in a ssouri state court. Then it went to the ssouri Supreme Court, the highest court Missouri. Because his case involved re than Missouri laws, his lawyers next nt to federal court. The final court was U.S. Supreme Court. It is the highest rt in the country.

19

Fighting Behind the Scenes

Dred Scott's case had become famous. People in the North still thought he had a strong case. But Scott's lawyers were worried. Would politics, rather than the law, decide the case?

There are nine **justices**, or judges, on the United States Supreme Court. The president nominates a person for a place on the Supreme Court. Then the Senate votes on whether to approve the person. Of the nine justices who heard Scott's case, seven were nominated by presidents from slave states. Five of the nine justices came from families that owned slaves.

It's a Fact

Separation of powers is built into the U.S. Constitution. There are three branches of government. The legislative branch is Congress. It makes the laws. The executive branch is the president. The president enforces the laws. The courts make up the judicial branch. They interpret the laws, or decide what they mean. The courts decide conflicts about the law. The Supreme Court can rule that a law passed by Congress is unconstitutional. That means it is no longer a valid law.

▲ James Buchanan was elected president in 1856. He unfairly influenced the Supreme Court in the Scott case.

The chief justice was Roger B. Taney. Taney was from Maryland, a slave state. He had been chief justice since 1836. He was near the end of his career.

People opposed to slavery wondered how fair the Court would be. James Buchanan was elected president in November 1856. He urged several justices to support the views of Chief Justice Taney. The justices did.

The U.S. Constitution calls for each branch of government to act separately. This is called the **separation of powers**. Buchanan clearly interfered in the workings of the Supreme Court in the case of *Scott v. Sandford*. What Buchanan did was against the law.

◀ Chief Justice Roger B. Taney

21

The Supreme Court Reaches a Decision

On March 6, 1857, the Supreme Court announced its decision in the Dred Scott case. By a vote of 7–2, the Court decided against Scott and in favor of John Sanford. Chief Justice Roger Taney wrote the Court's decision.

The Court ruled that Scott, as a slave, was not a citizen. Therefore, he did not have the right to sue for his freedom in court. Also, Scott belonged to Sanford. He was Sanford's property. He was not a person with the rights guaranteed in the Bill of Rights.

▲ Henry Clay is considered the author of the Missouri Compromise.

Taney's decision was a terrible loss for Scott. It also was a terrible loss for the anti-slavery movement. But Chief Justice Taney was not done. He also ruled that the Missouri Compromise was unconstitutional. That means the law went against the Constitution. Therefore, it was no longer in effect.

Taney wrote that the Missouri Compromise banned slavery in lands north of Missouri's southern border. Since Dred Scott was the personal property of John Sanford, the effect of the Missouri Compromise was to deny Sanford his property. Taney ruled that Congress could not make laws that took away people's right to their own property.

Professor David Blight on the Dred Scott Case:

Q. How did African Americans react to the Dred Scott case?

A. [After] the Dred Scott decision, [in the] spring of 1857, to be black in America was to live in the land of the Dred Scott decision, which, in effect, said, "You have no future in America." So, for the next three to three and a half years, down to the outbreak of the Civil War—and we must remember, nobody knew that war was coming when it was coming—to be black in America in the late 1850s was to live in a land that said you didn't have a future.

23

Reaction and Importance

The reaction to the Dred Scott decision was swift and fierce. Northern newspapers and political leaders were angry. Many pointed to the pro-slavery views of the justices on the Court. They spoke out against the justices for deciding the case on politics and not on the basis of law. Southerners were happy about the decision. They did not agree that politics or the judges' pro-slavery views were behind the decision.

THE DRED SCOTT DECISION:

SPEECH,

DELIVERED, IN PART, AT THE

ANNIVERSARY OF THE

AMERICAN ABOLITION SOCIETY,

HELD IN NEW YORK, MAY 14th, 1857.

In My Opinion

Northern and Southern newspapers had very different reactions to the Dred Scott decision.

1857
Evening Journal,
Albany, NY

March 9, 1857:
"The three hundred and forty-seven thousand five hundred and twenty-five Slaveholders in the Republic, accomplished day before yesterday a great success. . . . They converted the Supreme Court of the United States of America into . . . a court of human Slavery."

1857
Mercury,
Charleston, SC

March 17, 1857:
"The Supreme Court of the United States, in a recent case, has, by a decision of seven to two of the Judges, established as law what our Southern statesmen have been repeating daily for many years on the floors of Congress, that . . . slavery is guaranteed by the Constitution."

Abolitionists and African Americans turned to Frederick Douglass. He was an escaped slave and a great speaker. Douglass was widely respected among people fighting against slavery. Here is what Douglass said:

"You will ask . . . how I am affected by this devilish decision. My answer is, not thanks to the slaveholding wing of the Supreme Court—my hopes were never brighter than now. . . . Judge Taney can do many things . . . He may decide, and decide again . . . [but] he cannot change the essential nature of things—making evil good, and good, evil . . . The American people have been called upon . . . to abolish and put away the system of slavery . . . This decision, in my view, is a means of keeping the nation awake on the subject."

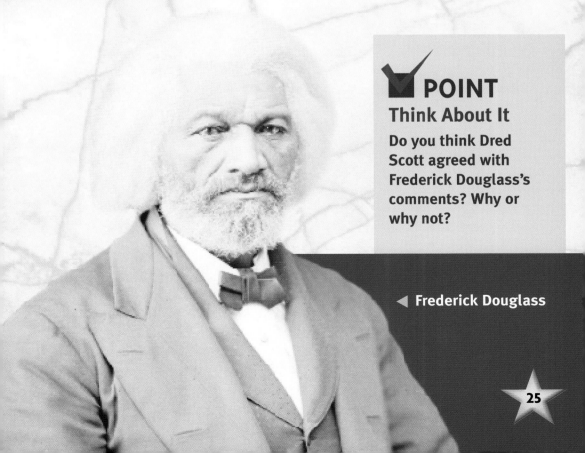

☑ POINT
Think About It
Do you think Dred Scott agreed with Frederick Douglass's comments? Why or why not?

◀ **Frederick Douglass**

The Division Between North and South Deepens

Chief Justice Taney had said that Congress could make no laws about slavery. This statement changed how both the North and the South viewed the slavery question forever. Henry Clay had died not long after his last great compromise in 1850. Belief in compromise vanished after the Dred Scott decision.

Eyewitness Account

"In [times past] our Declaration of Independence was held sacred by all, and thought to include all; but now, to aid in making slavery of the Negro universal and eternal, it is [attacked] . . . and torn, [so that the Founding Fathers would not even recognize it.]"

—Abraham Lincoln, in a speech given on June 26, 1857, about the Dred Scott case

Abolitionists had been trying to prevent slavery from moving into new territories and states. After the Dred Scott case, they worried that slavery might move into the North as well. Using Taney's logic, a case could be made that Northern laws against slavery would also be declared unconstitutional.

In the South, pro-slavery people were shocked and worried about the anger in the North. But they were firm about keeping their slaves. Many thought that it was no longer possible for Southern states to remain in the United States. Both the North and the South realized that the nation was running out of time to solve the crisis over slavery.

What Happened?

The Dred Scott case had a happy ending for Dred and Harriet Scott. Irene Emerson had remarried. Her husband, Dr. Calvin Chaffee, was a congressman from Massachusetts. He was also strongly against slavery. In 1857, Dred Scott was the most famous slave in America. Chaffee did not know that John Sanford's slave, Dred Scott, still belonged to his wife. Northern newspapers were quick to point out that Chaffee owned Dred Scott. The congressman had his wife return Dred and Harriet Scott to the Blow family. The Blows granted Dred and Harriet their freedom. After many long years and court battles, Dred Scott was finally free.

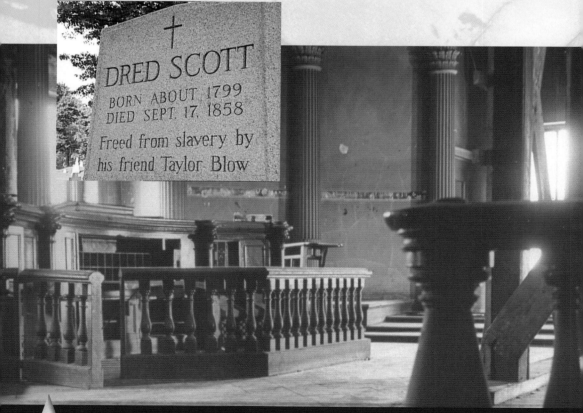

▲ St. Louis, Missouri, courtroom where Dred Scott trial took place

Dred Scott took a job working in a hotel in St. Louis. Sadly, he did not enjoy his freedom for long. Dred Scott died a year later, in 1858.

In 1860, Abraham Lincoln was elected president. Southern states had promised they would **secede** (sih-SEED), or withdraw, from the United States if that happened. The Civil War began a few months later. The question of slavery would finally be settled. But not before more than 600,000 Americans died in the bloodiest war ever fought by the United States.

In My Opinion

Chief Justice Roger B. Taney wrote the opinion of the seven justices who voted for the majority in the Dred Scott case. Justice Benjamin R. Curtis disagreed with the majority and wrote his own opinion, as did one other justice.

Chief Justice Roger B. Taney:
We hold these truths to be self-evident: that all men are created equal . . . [These] general words would seem to embrace the whole human family, . . . But it is . . . clear . . . that the enslaved African race were not intended to be included, and formed no part of the people who framed and adopted this declaration.

Justice Benjamin R. Curtis:
At the time of the Articles of Confederation [were voted on and approved], all free native-born [people living in] the States of New Hampshire, Massachusetts, New York, New Jersey, and North Carolina, though descended from African slaves, were not only citizens of those States, [but could vote and were] . . . on equal terms with other citizens.

I can find nothing in the Constitution which, . . . deprives of their citizenship any class of persons who were citizens of the United States at the time of its adoption, . . . or who should be native-born citizens of any State after its adoption.

29

Conclusion

Dred Scott was one of millions of African Americans who were enslaved. Scott tried to win his freedom by following the law. His case took eleven years. It went through four different courts. But the courts did not give justice to Dred Scott. Instead, politics, not laws, decided Dred Scott's case.

The case was an important event in the struggle to find a peaceful solution to the issue of slavery in the United States. In the end, a peaceful solution was not possible. The North and the South disagreed about slavery. Congress and the Supreme Court disagreed about slavery. War was the only way left to settle the issue.

Dred Scott did not live to see the end of slavery. But his brave fight for freedom played an important role in finally bringing the system of slavery to an end.

▲ The battle at Fort Sumter in Charleston, South Carolina, marked the start of the Civil War.

Glossary

abolitionist (a-buh-LIH-shun-ist) a person who worked to end slavery (page 4)

appeal (uh-PEEL) a request to have a legal case heard again by a higher court (page 14)

compromise (KAHM-pruh-mize) a settlement of differences reached by a consent of all (page 12)

crisis (KRY-sis) a dangerous or difficult situation (page 12)

free state (FREE STATE) a state where slavery was not allowed (page 7)

justice (JUS-tis) one of the nine judges on the United States Supreme Court (page 20)

lawsuit (LAW-soot) a case brought to a court of law (page 9)

plantation (plan-TAY-shun) a large farm (page 3)

secede (sih-SEED) to withdraw from a group or organization (page 29)

separation of powers (seh-puh-RAY-shun UV POW-erz) the idea in the United States Constitution that makes sure that none of the three branches of government is more powerful than the other two (page 21)

slave state (SLAVE STATE) a state where slavery was legal (page 7)

territory (TAIR-ih-tor-ee) a settled area belonging to the United States that is not yet a state (page 7)

Index

abolitionist, 4, 18, 25, 27

appeal, 14, 18

Blow family, 6, 14, 28

Buchanan, James, 21

Chaffee, Dr. Calvin, 28

Clay, Henry, 13, 26

compromise, 12–13, 23, 26

crisis, 12, 15, 27

Douglass, Frederick, 4, 25

Emerson, Irene Sanford, 8–9, 13–15, 18, 28

Emerson, John, 6–9, 13

free state, 7, 12

justice, 20–24, 26

lawsuit, 9–10

Lincoln, Abraham, 29

Missouri Compromise, 12–13, 23

Northwest Ordinance, 11

Northwest Territory, 11

plantation, 3

Sanford, John, 18–19, 22–23, 28

Scott, Dred, 5–15, 18–24, 28–30

Scott, Harriet Robinson, 8–9, 28

secede, 29

separation of powers, 21

slave state, 7, 12–13, 20–21

Stowe, Harriet Beecher, 17

Taney, Chief Justice Roger B., 21–23, 25–27

territory, 7, 9, 11, 13–14, 16–17, 27

Uncle Tom's Cabin, 17

U.S. Supreme Court, 5, 19–22, 25, 30